MW00895449

Shirley,

Thank you so much!

Be Blessed!!

What Daddy Should Have Told His Little Girl

Tony Gaskins, Jr.

11-9-09

SokheChapke Publishing

Published by:
SokheChapke Publishing, Inc.
P. O. Box 21161   Tallahassee, FL 32316
541 E. Tennessee Street   Tallahassee, FL 32308
Phone: 1-866-711-5984
Website: http:www.sokhechapkepublishing.com
(Previous edition published by Soul Writers, LLC)

Library Of Congress Catalog Number:
ISBN-10: 0-9793451-7-0
ISBN-13: 978-0-9793451-7-3

First Edition
First Printing, December 2007
10 9 8 7 6 5 4 3 2 1

Published and printed in the
United States Of America

Cover design and formatting created by:
Renaissance Consulting Services
website: http:www.rcsteched.com

Dedication

Lou Emma Jamison
Cathy Gaskins
Latesha Gaskins
Sheri Chanroo Gaskins
Joslyn Giles
Adrienne Blake
Andrea Woodfolk
Alex Dukes (R. I. P.)

TABLE OF CONTENTS

INTRODUCTION

Every woman wants to know what goes on inside a man's head. The same goes for every man regarding women. In fact, we all dream of seeing life through our opposite's eyes. If that were possible, however, we would be able to understand the things they do and why they are the way that they are.

This book allows a woman to see life through a man's eyes. It is intended to break down the barriers that exist between men and women; and to help women clearly understand how and *why* some men behave the way they do.

A major objective of this book is to give women a better chance at relationships; to give women a tough skin for the battle ahead when dealing with men. On the other hand, this book is not meant to degrade men in any way, but instead challenges every man who reads this to be a better man. A man is not a man if he cannot admit to his faults and search for a solution to make himself better. Another purpose of this book is to save young women from the pain and agony that comes with dating and falling in love. You may say it's life, but I don't believe life is justified by the amount of pain a person suffers.

I have sat on the sidelines and watched women very dear to me get played, abused, tricked, and deceived; consequently, I vowed to educate as many young women as possible on the ups and downs of relationships and the ways of men.

In the case of men, it's OK to play games as long as someone they really care about never gets hurt. Then, as soon as they see their little sister or mother suffer the wrongs of a man, they immediately wish there were things they could do to change it.

This book is my step in the right direction. It may not reach every young woman's hand, and it may not leave much of an impression in the hearts and minds of everyone who reads it, but if I am able to enlighten one woman and offer guidance for enabling her relationship to be a fulfilling one, then my job is done.

This book will cover ten very important questions that often resonate in the hearts of women. Each chapter has a different question. In response to these questions, my answers are very explicit, providing the most detailed answers possible.

I'm very confident with the answers

that I provide in each chapter. I not only took notes while observing other men in their actions towards women, but in most cases I am actually the man that these women are referring to in the chapter questions. Therefore, the answers will likely be very closely related to some of the issues the readers of this book may be facing in their own relationships. The answers are not long or drawn out; instead, they are very specific. Read the answers that relate to you first, and then read the rest to enhance your own knowledge.

So I say to the young women who end up reading this book, as you embark on life's journey, my wish is that you will open your mind, as well as your heart. Take heed to what you read. Many women say, "Oh, not my man," or "That's just his opinion," and that's the worst way you can think. I'm here today because I listened and I let those that went before me blaze the trail; that way, all I would have to do is walk and not faint. I encourage you to walk and not faint. To all my sisters who read this book, this is from my heart, and I hope it reaches yours.

STATISTICS

Divorce:

Many Americans live alone. The United States leads the world in one-person households. The United States has the world's highest marriage rate - as well as the world's highest divorce rate. Two-third of all black marriages end in divorce.

Young couples may be together for months, not decades, as divorce occurs progressively earlier. Even though the divorce rate actually leveled off in the 1990s (from about 50% of new marriages to about 43% currently), a 2001 survey by the Centers for Disease Control and Prevention says 20% of divorces in first marriages now occur within five years.

http://www.uploadexperience.com/ statistics.htm

Statistics Regarding Interracial Dating/ Marriage:

The frequency of interracial dating among American youth has dramatically increased. According to some recent studies, as many as 57 % of teenagers have dated someone outside of their race. An additional 30 % have indicated that they would consider dating outside of their race.
http://www.enotes.com/ interracial-relationships-article/
Seventy-two percent of black and white couples are composed of a minority husband and a white wife.
http://www.isteve.com/ Articles_Interracial_Marriage.htm

Statistics Regarding Abuse:

• Every 9 seconds, a woman is battered in the U.S.
• Approximately 95% of the victims of domestic violence are women. *(U. S. Department of Justice)*

Fifty percent of all women murdered in the United States are killed by a spouse or an acquaintance. *(Journal of Trauma, 1992)*

Statistics Regarding Cheating:

Statistics suggest that 40% of women and 60% of men at one point indulge in extramarital affairs.

It's estimated that 80% of marriages will have one partner at one point or another involved in marital infidelity.
http://www.catch-a-cheating-wife.com/

CHAPTER 1

Why is it that Some Men Don't Value Celibacy?

If a man really likes you and cares about who you are and what you want, then he'll respect your wishes; however, if he only cares about himself and his personal needs, then more than likely he will not accept celibacy. Every woman should ask the man they are interested in about his feelings toward celibacy. This way you will see exactly what his intentions are, or at least some signs of them. A genuine man or a relationship-oriented man will wait for you. He may apply a little pressure, but he'll wait. If a man says that he can't wait because he's a grown man and his body is accustomed to sex, then he's in it for himself. Or if he says that abstention from sex will cause medical problems, he's in it for himself. There are no harmful side effects that come along with celibacy. Watch out for the deep explanation that sex will bring you two closer and allow him to express feelings for you that words can't achieve. That's a man who's used to dealing in this way, and women usually fall for it. I know a lot of men, including myself, who have been successful with that line after it has been applied just right.

One problem with practicing celibacy with a man you've just met is that he may see you as a goal. It would be very easy to discern between a man that is genuine and a man that is goal-driven. One difference would be the time factor. If he's genuine, he'll spend all the time he can getting to know you and asking questions about you while building trust. On the other hand, a goal-oriented man's topic of conversation will be about sex; or your reasons for choosing celibacy. His phone calls will come few and far between, and when you finally talk to each other the conversations will be short. Even though a man is goal-driven, that doesn't mean he can't wait, and, in fact, he may wait a long time for you. He can even wait months but his time will be divided between you and other interests. He won't give you all of his time. He may get in touch with you when it is convenient for him, and this may very well cause you to think he really likes you when he's actually just waiting for you to give in. On the other hand, a genuine man will talk with you or spend everyday with you getting to know you quickly with no reference to sex at all.

Be careful if you believe you're his goal! Play your cards right. Don't start pretending to be one thing, and then turn out to be another. It is important to make a man earn his keep by staying strong in your beliefs, and, even if he's out to get you, you will be the winner if you hold out and don't give him sex. When you finally decide to have sex with him, he should have invested so much time that he never wants to leave you because he's so deeply in love. One thing men often forget is that when they play with fire they can get burned. Many think they can engage in deep conversations with you, go on dates, and still keep their heart distant from love. So, while he's waiting for you to give him your innocence, his goal is to not bond with you emotionally. However, if you save that ace card, that handsome young goal-seeking man will fall in love with you and share the best of his love with yours.

Here is my point. If you decide on celibacy, make sure you don't change your mind before knowing beyond the shadow of a doubt that he will do anything for you. Never use celibacy to get brownie points as a classy lady. If it's not what you really want, or how you really are, don't fake it. If you do, you are playing yourself! As soon as you say you're celibate, the man immediately goes into game mode. He'll bide his time and stay distant if he's not sincere. He won't call everyday, and he won't talk for very long when he does ring your phone. *Why?* Because he doesn't want to give much of himself if he's getting nothing in return. When a man plays this role, it's because he is focusing on the women in his life who satisfy his sexual appetite and calling you when his other women can't be reached. The crazy thing is, usually when a man plays this role, the woman falls for him. *Why?* It's human nature to want what you can't have, or to want someone who doesn't want you.

As a woman, you should understand that when a man you've just met calls you three or four times a day, the man seems pushy. Just like the laws of physics, if he pushes toward you, then you move in the opposite direction. But when he plays it cool and pulls away, it draws you closer to him. Strange but true. That is why women are known for falling for the bad guys or the thugs. A man with a demanding schedule, like the life that comes with the streets, doesn't have much time for you. A certain part of you will respond to that because you have the freedom you need and you don't have to be bothered all the time. At the same time, you begin to long for that man. You question yourself, "Why isn't he feeling me – Is it because I'm not giving it up?" His absence makes your heart grow fonder. To question yourself is the worst thing you can do. If he doesn't call, then you know right away he's not serious. Never think he's too busy. No matter what a man has to do, if he likes you he can make time for you. If he doesn't come to you, then don't chase him. If he only calls you every other day, don't give in thinking that it's because you aren't good enough or that he doesn't like you. Stay steadfast in your decision on celibacy and force him to play by your rules. Soon you'll see his true colors.

Most men practice what I call the three-month rule. The average player or "go getter" won't wait longer than that. A player may wait a month, and if you haven't given it up yet, then most likely he will move on. But if you show signs of weakness, as if you're getting closer to giving in, then that will keep him around a little longer, and he'll start playing at a distance. So, stay just as strong as you were on the day you decided to be celibate.

On the other hand, if a man has been talking to you EVERYDAY, and you reach the three-month mark, I would bet my bottom dollar he is for real. Meaning he isn't obligated to another woman whole-heartedly, and, if he has one, he is willing to leave her for you. He also respects your decisions, as well as respect you as a person. Of course, that doesn't mean he's not having sex. A man will easily respect your wishes to be celibate, but that does not mean he has the same standards for himself. Therefore, he may be fulfilling his lust or sexual appetite elsewhere. You can never be 100% sure about anything, but, as they say, time will tell. To test men, use no other weapon but TIME. Blessed are those who wait and cursed are those who rush. That goes to say that a man who can wait has a good heart;

although he is not perfect, he can be molded. A man who is in it for himself or just out to cheat on his girlfriend or wife won't waste much time on you. I say all that to say, DON'T PLAY YOURSELF!

CHAPTER 2

Why is it So Hard for a Man to Express his Feelings?

What a lot of women don't know is that when a man falls in love he almost never falls out of love. A woman has a built-in recovery system, unlike a man. Therefore, a man protects his heart in a different way. Women can cry without shame or remorse. A man doesn't feel the same freedom to cry through his problems. Crying isn't manly in our society; thus, in order not to end up crying, a man can't allow himself to get hurt. A man will hide his feelings as long as he can. For a woman to know a man loves her, she should feel it and not hear it. A good slogan to live by is "Believe none of what you hear and only half of what you see." I recommend this rule because everything a man tells you may not be from his heart.

When trying to understand a man's feelings, make sure you tread lightly. This is a *Pandora's Box* of information that I hesitate to open because you may not want to know what is really inside.

We've all heard of the *poker face* in a card game. When playing poker, one is taught not to let his expressions show what type of hand he has or the next move he intends to make. The same concept applies to a man who is involved in a relationship. As men, we try to hide our emotions so that our women never know how we truly feel. That way they always have to try to understand us, and as long as they are trying to do so we do not have to worry about them leaving. Therefore, a man will stretch this process as long as possible until he knows for a fact she is in love.

My father always told me that a woman is patient enough to play a role all the way up until married. Then as soon as she gets that ring of security, everything about her changes. When you think about it in other walks of life, this is very true.

Imagine fighting for a position at work or on a team. While you're fighting for that spot you give your all and nothing less. You always try to outperform those around you so that you look better than they do. Then you finally win the spot you wanted so badly and realize there is no competition because you are exactly where you wanted to be. Eventually, you start to slack, you don't try as hard as you used to, and you don't give the energy and dedication you used to. A man has this theory down to a science. As a man, our defense mechanism is to hide our feelings and never let the woman know she can relax because we aren't going anywhere.

On the other hand, a man may not be telling you how he feels because he feels absolutely nothing. While a woman is being sincere and taking it all in, the man is brushing it off as just another day. As men, we try not to sit and fantasize about marriage with kids and the deepest love. We inherently know that if we fall in love it will take more than a disaster to make us fall out of love. Therefore, knowing that's the case, we try our best to fight love for as long as we can. As a woman, you may feel the world for the man you're with and wonder everyday why he doesn't express his feelings or write you a letter telling you how he feels. The reason is that he likes you so he doesn't want to lie to you. He knows it's a good possibility that, if he does, he could end up hurting you since he's not ready for love. So, he says nothing at all. When you wonder why your man isn't telling you how he feels, don't always brush it off as if he doesn't know how to; instead, understand that he is probably trying to understand and sort out his own feelings. As a man, I would say it takes twice as long for us to fall in love. I've had relationships in which I didn't truly begin to love until after a year, but they loved me from the second month. Men and women feel things differently for a reason, and the reason will be discussed in this, and other chapters in this book as well.

Consider this scenario. Your man could be starting to like you, but he's holding back. He takes bad feelings from past relationships and recycles them to you. This man may write poems and letters with deep meanings, but in essence, you don't believe that his feelings are sincere yet. The thing is, he knows he has to express something because you're giving so much of yourself to the relationship. If he doesn't give you something back, then you'll feel like he doesn't like you. Truthfully speaking, he knows you are wife material but he really doesn't want to let you know that. Nonetheless, there is something about his expressions that indicates he's not being real. You sense that he is just spittin' game with his words or letters, but you can't just accuse him of that, so you accept it one word at a time. The reason some men fake it, is that they are not really feeling much yet. Your man knows you are pretty and that you have a nice body with all the features he likes, but that's all physical. For a long time, your man will have a hard time pinpointing exactly what it is about you that he likes outside of your looks. All along, you are falling head over heels for him because you're judging his qualities and not his looks.

You will eventually find yourself shutting other men out and walking with your head in the clouds. Your man will see it in your eyes and feel it in your touch that you are truly focused on him. There is probably nothing he could ask for that you wouldn't do your best to get it. Be careful; when a man begins to feel like this, he may put you to the test. This may scare him a little so he'll back away and begin to treat you like a fling. He may not call everyday or he may wait for you to call him. After a little while, you will begin to ask yourself if he even likes you as much as you initially thought. He will also wait as long as possible to reveal his deepest feelings, which would in turn, keep you satisfied as his woman. Just know that if this happens to you, this is when a man is guarding his heart. He knows that if you are feeling detached, then it's time for him to demonstrate his feelings more openly in order to keep you. If he's smart, he'll muster up genuine feelings and express them to you. Most likely, since this is what you've been waiting on, you'll buy right into them and that will be a smart move on your part. But at the same time, he will continue to ignore the love that is forming so that it doesn't get the best of him. He knows you're falling in love, but he won't let himself fall for you in order to keep the upper hand. This man won't calculate the things you do for him because that would make him love you back. He'll sit back and act as if nothing is going on and let you fall deeper in love. While you're changing everything to perfection for him, he's sitting and watching every minute of it because emotionally he's not there yet. Some females go as far as getting the guy's name tattooed on themselves in an intimate place, and deleting all the other guys' numbers from their phones even if they were just friends. So, if that's you, please believe you're not alone.

You may have done all of the above and still not know his true feelings about you. Think back and ask yourself if your man was just all words, and you were the one with all the actions. If that proves to be the case, then he knows for sure that you love him with all your heart and if he leaves, you'd be heartbroken because of the many things that you have sacrificed. However, if you were the one to leave, you may not know if he truly misses you. This is the security that every man wants, and this is why men hold back. He wants to know you love him and wants you to think he loves you. Therefore, he feels that if he shows that he loves you too, you'll stop doing the things you did to get him there. Most likely, he's right and even you know that.

So, you may read this and realize that you have experienced this before, or have seen it happen to others. A man never wants to reveal his true feelings, especially early on in a relationship. In his mind, his feelings are money in the bank. He will continue to tell you just what you need to hear to give you the security that you've already given him. You see, this is a man's defense mechanism. Your man will hide his feelings because he's ashamed to let you know you got him whipped. He knows that when it's real, you will know its real and that's when you won't have to keep trying. The logic is simple. Once you reach a goal, you no longer have to continue striving toward it.

Additionally, although it sounds crazy, when a man truly likes or loves a woman, he won't express his true feelings because he doesn't want to lose her. Where men mess up is when they go too long without expressing their feelings, and they let her slip away; but that's another book in itself! As a woman, beware of a man who fills your head with poems and love letters. A lot of times when he is writing to you, it's because he knows that's what you want, but to the contrary, he may not feel that way at all. When a man holds back, and you don't know what he feels (but a part of you can feel it), that's when you should cherish it. It is at that moment, when a man is most likely sincere and genuine. Knowledge is power, and power turns into pride, and pride comes before a fall. This is an unwritten law but every man's heart is programmed that way.

To every woman who reads this: know your man! Don't wait on words because those same spoken words could be without substance. Believe in his actions. Silently, actions speak louder than words. Look for a man's actions, because that is how you will know he loves you. The Bible says you'll know the tree by the fruit it bears. A grapefruit tree won't produce oranges, and an orange tree won't produce a grapefruit. That goes to say a good man won't make you feel bad, and a bad man won't make you feel good. So, in watching for a man's actions, look for the man who will hold your hand in public, the man who will rub your back until you fall asleep, and the man who will cook breakfast for you in the morning. The amount of money a man spends on you and the nice places a man takes you means nothing. Those things require nothing of that man, but a man who gives of himself, a man who sacrifices his own time and feelings for yours, well that's the man who has real feelings. Many women focus on the wrong things in a relationship and let the little things pass them by. It takes more of a man to get up and cook breakfast for you in the morning than it does for him to take you to a four-star restaurant. If a man doesn't love you, then he won't give of HIMSELF. It's important that you are able to tell the difference between a man giving of HIMSELF and a man just giving.

As a woman, you should respect yourself as one respects a priceless piece of art. Honor yourself as a virtuous woman and never give into insecurities and let your guard down. Don't ever feel like you owe a man anything. A man knows he has to work to get what he wants in any area of his life, and this is true for successful relationships as well. Many women give in to a man because he buys flowers or spends money at the mall. He does it because he knows it will make you feel obligated or owe him something in return. Since you don't have the money, you may repay him with sex or some type of intimacy. This is not necessary, and a man does not respect a woman who pays him back in that way. Respect yourself by letting him go to the moon and back, and not giving him anything sexual as repayment. If you are not personally asking for his time or his gifts, then you do not owe him anything in return.

Many men will see you as a challenge, and, as men, that's what we live for. It is a man's nature to fight, challenge, bet, and take chances. Look into history all over the world. Across the globe, men have had duels, battles, and all types of mono y mono competitions to prove who the better man is.

Although this proves nothing at all, in society it has been seen as a test of masculinity. Such is the same when it comes to women. If you jokingly say to a man, "I'm practicing celibacy", that man sees a challenge. He then will set in his mind that he is going to accept this challenge and not give up until he is successful with ending your personal promise to be celibate. Then the game begins. You go on dates, to the movies, and out to eat. You talk on the phone for hours and visit one another on occasion. You know in your heart you'll give into sex if he pushes the right buttons while whispering the perfect lines.

Let's say it's been two and a half months. You're reaching your three-month goal, but you're blinded so you can't tell if he's sincere or goal-driven. You try to play it safe, but you'll crash by default if what comes out of your mouth doesn't line up with what is in your heart. Since he's goal-driven, he's being patient – and one night he gets you in the right place. Let's say you've finally let him come over after midnight. Remember, you've been claiming celibacy but you didn't mean it, you just wanted to seem classy. He sits and watches TV a little and talks to you softly and passes a few jokes.

Then he asks about your day. You indulge in his false sincerity and open up very comfortably. He moves a little closer and puts his hand on your thigh. You see where it's going, but you think nothing of it. Then he leans in and kisses your neck. "Ooo, that feels good", you say to yourself. He does it again as he rubs his hands up and down your thigh. He eases in-between your thighs with his hand and heads straight to the spot. Before you know it, your shorts are coming off, you lose control because it's late, it's dark, and it is feeling so good. He has you exactly where he wants you and you have given in to him. At this point, he knows it's going down. He pleases you the best way he knows how and he knows you have reached the point of no return. All your inhibitions are out the window. No matter what, you've gone too far.

This encounter may not last long enough to send you up a wall, or it may be so short it leaves you wanting more. But guess what, it doesn't matter anymore because YOU JUST PLAYED YOURSELF! Then, you noticed the haste in his departure and eventually the decrease in his calls and the change of content in the conversations you share, because this man was goal-driven.

Once a man achieves one goal, then logically new ones are set. A goal-oriented man will either leave you alone after that sexual encounter or set new goals for you. That goal may have been just to have sex, but the next may be to have sex unprotected or on demand with you. The positions and the locations can be individual goals also. Please know a man's mind won't venture too far in this goal-setting process. A catchy phrase in one ethnic community relating to this is, "Wam! Bam! Thank you, Ma'am!" Appropriate, huh?

Remember, when traveling an avenue of respect, make sure that whatever comes out of your mouth lines up with what's inside your heart. Be sincere about what you say you are or what you are striving to be. Don't hold out for the fun of it because if you really want him you're going to give in, and then the battle is lost. A one-night stand can be on the first night or it can be after the first night you give up your innocence to the man. If that's what the man wants, then that is what he will accomplish. So, don't play with fire if you don't want to get burned. Celibacy is a choice, and a noble one at that. Don't use the word in vain or your time will be in vain. Don't go to the point of no return because at that point you are either going to give it willingly or he is going to take it (date rape?).

CHAPTER 3

Can Guys and Girls be "Just Friends?"

Of course, many people will read this and say, "Yes." On the contrary, my answer is, "No," and I have done surveys to prove that my theory is true. Personally, I do not believe in male and female "friendships;" because they always turn out to have some type of benefits. Today, the phrase "Friends with benefits" has emerged as commonplace, especially in our society because people start out as friends and end up being more than that. Don't get me wrong, I do believe that the greatest foundation for any relationship is friendship. "Love without friendship as its foundation is like a mansion built on the sand". So, I am very much in favor of cross-gender friendships; in fact, I would search for that if I were looking for a good relationship. Men cannot be genuine friends with females due to our *predator mentality*, and the only exception to that rule is if the woman isn't attractive in any way. Literally, the woman would have to be in a vegetative state for her male friend not to be attracted to her at any time.

I asked ten different women if they've ever had male friends. All ten said, "Yes" at one point in their life. Then I asked them if the men ever made sexual passes at them, and all ten said, "Yes" at one time or another. Some women said it took years before they did, but it never failed. In life we live by margins. Majority rules, therefore with statistics we go by what the majority says. Yes, there may be a few men who can be strictly friends, but even if that were the case, those men most likely don't like women. Those are the only true male friends, and I'm sure that many women have had that homosexual male friend at one point. I've met those types of guys before, and they are just like females when it comes down to the way they carry themselves and the way they think. Since they are attracted to males, they can be strictly friends with females. In essence, it's just like a female having another female as her friend because the homosexual male friend may think and act just as her girlfriends does.

A lot of men play the friend role to get a woman. In my opinion, it's the best role to play. It works better than the taken role, better than the gangster role, and better than the baller role.

Beware of a man when he say's he just wants to be a friend. Here's how it goes: a man will introduce himself to you in a pleasant manner or is introduced to you in a harmless and calm setting. This man will engage you in conversation that's all about you, knowing that, as a woman, sometimes you just need someone to listen to you. He will go out to eat with you and chill with you in intimate settings but never attempt intimacy. He'll say nice things and be the sweetest gentleman, never expressing a sexual comment or while trying to flirt. He'll seem just like a brother figure. Before you know it, you'll find yourself confiding in him and trusting him with your every secret and thought. This is when he knows he has you on the ropes. If you get caught up in this, you'll either get played for a fool or you'll meet the man of your dreams. Personally, I don't believe any man just wants to be friends. He sees you as prey but he knows in order to get you he may have to stalk you in the proper way. He will lay low and play his hand right while waiting for the right time to make his move. You will find yourself opening up and letting your guard down. You'll share friendly hugs and walks in the park and things of that nature. All the while, you are growing fonder of this gentleman. Then you begin to form a trust in your friendship, and this is when you are almost gone. The man will take his time. For different men, it's different periods of time before he makes his move. For example, a quiet and reserved schoolboy could wait a year or more, but an outgoing and go-getter type of man may wait two months. His ultimate goal is to make you feel so comfortable that you throw yourself at him. If he is handsome or smooth enough, he knows that he is capable of doing this. Now, if he isn't used to getting girls on demand, then he knows he will have to wait until you are so comfortable with him that when he does make a move you will entrust your body to him without hesitation. That's when it is hardest for you as a woman. *Why?* Because he has been so nice to you all of this time that even when he makes a pass it doesn't seem as threatening, so you let it slide. What you will notice is that each new pass will get a little more aggressive, and, if you don't stop him, it'll end with you two being very intimate. This is where "Friends with benefits" begin. A lot of women just want a male friend to get the male perspective on life or help her with her man. And a lot of men will play that role just waiting for the day that you are down and out because your man has finally slipped up and broken your heart. Then he'll move in as the sweet and innocent Prince Charming, and, since you're in a vulnerable state of mind, you most likely will give in to his charm.

I'm sure you can remember the time this may have happened to you, or almost happened to you. Just like the ten women I interviewed, you may have gone through this same experience.

If you are the least bit attractive, no man can be just your friend. He can try to, and he may last a long time, but he will eventually make his move. No matter how long it takes, don't get caught up in the amount of time he's invested without trying you. Just know that in many cases, some men view women as prey, and, just like every predator, a man takes his time when the prey they want is very hard to catch! It's usually the beautiful or very classy women men try to befriend in order for them to let their guards down. If a woman has ever been told she is pretty in any way, shape, or form, then that woman should automatically know that she can not befriend a man. Stay alert!

There are perks to having male friends, though, so please don't just push him away, even though you may suspect he doesn't want to be a genuine friend. Many relationships are physical. Yet, after the sex becomes boring and looks begin to fade, you may both realize that there is nothing left to stand on. However, when you have friendship as your foundation, you always have something to fall back on. In short, if a man tries to be your friend allow him to do so, but put him through the test. Don't let his little passes slip by, and don't allow yourself to fall for him too soon. Be strong and stay focused because a handsome friend could very easily turn into Prince Charming. You know very well that there is no better feeling than having someone who is attractive and whom you can call on whenever you have a problem. You should be able to sit and talk and laugh with him for hours; to feel like you are safe and that he is on your side. You want to feel that with him you'll never have to worry about arguing, being beaten, or being cheated on. That's the greatest feeling in the world. Everyone wants that type of friend. This is why this type of friendship may be rewarding. When a man has to pay his dues and he has to befriend you before he can become intimate with you, then he appreciates you as a woman.

When a man has to put in genuine time and he is willing to do so, that means that he is serious about what he is doing. When he finally gets you, (if he ever gets you) he will appreciate you more than ever. You are his work of art; what you have is not something he bought or found on the street corner. In the relationship, there is something you've built together--and a man appreciates that more. Realistically, if you put a man to the test, he is forced to be genuine and forced to truly get to know you as a person before anything physical happens, and he will love you for that. Long and healthy relationships are formed in this manner, and this is why I believe in building a friendship before starting a physical relationship. A man who has to build something from the ground up will appreciate it much more than if just given to him. So when you meet a man, and he wishes to befriend you, make him build a relationship with you from the ground up. Don't give him anything; instead make him earn it. That way, if you ever decide to submit to this man regardless of his first intentions, he will be hooked. This is the method that you as a woman can find the love of your life. So many women make the mistake of just letting a man into their lives by allowing him to claim them right off. Whereas, when the man has paid his dues, he comes to understand what real love is about. Love after friendship is not guaranteed, nor is it forever, but it is better to have loved and lost than to have never loved at all. My mother always told me, "The best of friends make the best of lovers". This meant so much to me after I found it to be true. When you have someone whom you can just sit and laugh and talk with and never have to worry about kissing and touching or having sex, that is when you've found something special. Then, when you are old and tired and you have no desire to make love to that person, you both will still enjoy each other's company because you are able to be friends.

If you have a male friend, and you have asked yourself this same question, "Can guys and girls be just friends?", then I would urge you to ask him the same question.

Communication is the key. Ask your male friend if he likes you. Remember he's being your friend to wait you out, to draw you to him. In a sense, he is the predator and you are the prey! He is being your friend to reverse the role and make you want him. So ask him, "Friend, do you like me?" See what he says and go from there. Most of the time, he will be honest with you because this is what he wants. He wants you to wonder about these things, and he wants you to want these things. So, if you ask him, then you are allowing him the opportunity to be real with you. Make sure you have a real friendship when you ask him. For example, don't ask after the first week or two; instead, wait a month or so; a sufficient amount of time to build a friendship that can go places.

When you allow him to open up, you are allowing your friendship to grow in the right direction. When you know what you are dealing with, you know what to expect; and this is one thing that you can expect a man to be honest about. He wants honesty all along. If he says he doesn't like you, then he's lying, and you know that you asked too early, so back off and give it a little while longer. When he says, "No," it doesn't mean he doesn't like you; it just means he's not ready to admit it. So, in this case, time is of the essence. When you give a man time to build up feelings, it's only a matter of time before he explodes. So if you ask him before he makes a fool of himself, then you've saved yourself a good friend and some embarrassment.

After he's admitted to liking you, just continue in the same direction you were already moving, knowing and understanding that you are building something that can last a lifetime. Trust me, when a relationship is built on friendship it steps into a whole different realm of love, and it has to be evaluated differently from a relationship built on lust. Therefore, many of the answers in this book may not be precisely for a relationship built on friendship. However, when you build on this foundation you are building a mansion that can be passed down the line. This is not conventional love, this is unconditional love. So continue what you have with your male friend and don't blame him when he is weakened by the overwhelming power of friendship. A powerful friendship has made many a man and woman like their own kind, so imagine what it can do if it's with the opposite sex.

Cherish what you have and know that

if you play it smoothly and take your time, allowing love to take its natural course, then you will discover the greatest love you can ever have. If you just want a friend, and you do not wish for this man to ever be your lover, then I suggest you have an open mind when befriending the opposite sex or just stick to female friends. Sometimes looks and money aren't what's best for you. True love has no face, and its value is priceless, meaning that no amount of money can buy true love. And when you least expect it, the ugliest or poorest man in the world could make you feel like the most important individual on Earth just by being your friend. So be safe and be smart when it comes to befriending a man. Don't be afraid to just let it flow. In life, you may go up and down or in and around. You may have kids and marriages. A good friend will always be there. You never know when that seed of loving friendship will blossom and you'll reap your harvest. Be safe and be blessed!

CHAPTER 4

Why is there a double standard between men and women regarding sex?

Just like the answer to almost any question, the answer to this one lies in history. A wise man once said, "There is nothing new under the sun." In this day and time, unwritten laws are the same as they were in the past. My mother put it best, "When it comes to the number of partners a woman has had to the number of partners a man has had, you have the zero and the hero." That statement is as simple as this: if a woman has numerous partners in our society, she is a zero, but if a man has many partners he is the hero.

I am a firm believer in combining one's history and one's biography to find the makeup of that person. In this case, it would be the history of mankind plus the biography of each gender to find the makeup of males and females. If we take a close look at history (his-story), we will find the answer to this question, as well as why this double-edged sword has stabbed at the heart of societies across the globe. There seems to be a universal law that suggests sex is a sacred act for a woman, and almost like a job for a man. Even in certain religions, such as Islam, a man may have more than one wife, but to each wife he is the only husband. Every culture is different. However, let's consider this issue more deeply.

According to Biblical teachings, men were created in the image of God and women were created as helpmates to the man. Therefore, in order to populate the word, it was up to the man to be *fruitful and multiply*. A woman could not conceive a child any other way except by a man. Let's look a little deeper. We begin with Adam and Eve, and they begat Cain and Able. Then Cain killed Able. Already, you have two men and one woman. It was up to them to create more of their own kind. That, in essence, would consist of brothers and sisters sleeping together and one man sleeping with many women to impregnate them, since the ratio of men to women wasn't equal and it would never be. If you notice in the genealogy of the Bible, women weren't listed. It reads that Adam begat Seth and Seth begat Enos and Enos begat Cainan and so on and so on. To further emphasize the point, laws that govern our nation did not even include women as equals. The man was, and to some extend still is considered the ruler, the head, or whatever royal title that was conveyed upon him. Remember, during Biblical times, replenishing the earth generation after generation was a job. It was a duty given to man by God. He said go forth and be fruitful. This was a direct order from God to man to replenish the earth with his own likeness. Fathers would have to sleep with daughters to keep the line going. As disgusting as it may seem to people of our time, this is what we are taught. Imagine this, a man not only sleeping with his wife, but his daughter and his granddaughters. According to Biblical stories, a brother not only slept with his sisters but also his nieces. This is how our world began. From the beginning of time, you see the patterns of men sleeping with numerous women to reproduce as many of his likeness as he could. This was socially accepted and obviously appreciated in that time.

I would like to remind you of the story in the Bible about Abraham and Sarah. God promised Abraham a child, but Sarah could not bear children for many years; therefore, Sarah instructed Abraham to partake in this "sacred" act with the handmaid. Abraham did so, and they produced an offspring of their own. It doesn't end there. Abraham still went back to Sarah and continued trying, and finally God's promise was fulfilled, and they begat Isaac. Once again, you see a man of God sleeping with numerous women for the cause of mankind. I repeat, a man of God. According to the Bible, this is what women expected and accepted. Also in that time, Kings had a Queen and many other wives too. A King was known to have as many as a thousand wives. This meant that, by our calendar year, a King could sleep with a different woman every day for over two whole years. It gets deeper. Not only could he have that many wives, but he would have around 300 concubines. These women weren't even wives; these were like *"women on the side"* as we would refer to them today. You see, in this present day, we are living in the furthest, most diluted version of what was harmless and accepted in the days of old. The answer lies within history. Now, are you beginning to see the double standard?

As time went on, different races and regions would disagree on this subject and make laws that oftentimes prohibited a man from having more than one wife. An average man wasn't granted that privilege, or at least it was not often recorded. Today we know that there are no Kings in our country, and a President is as close as we come to having a king. There is no clause in our laws that allow him to have more than one wife. In fact, the only thing that may allow multiple wives is ones' religion, and in our nation those particular religions do not dominate our political structure. Our nation is built on Christian foundations, where a man belongs to a woman and a woman belongs to a man. Once entered into holy matrimony, not only is it a sin but it is against the law to sleep outside of that marriage. One would ask, "Why is it still seen as OK for a man to sleep with many women?" In a sense, it's a goal to see how many they can sleep with. The answer is simple: although laws have changed, the heart of man is still the same.

Until God can change the heart of a man, it will always remain the same. Now in this day and age, we see a more vulgar use of a man's body. But because of the laws we have in place it seems as if the double standard should no longer apply. Here's what happened. The essence of reproduction was lost, just like the essence of sex itself was lost over time. We began with men and women and now we have gays and lesbians. Overtime, the essence of everything that God set in motion will be lost and replaced with a new more rebellious rampage without cause. Similar to how we came about Sodom and Gomorrah, through evolution, we will eventually leave out the blueprint that it began with and revert to a modern day rendition of what it used to be. When we think about sex and the double standard, we realize there shouldn't still be one since there is no need for reproduction. The world has now been over populated, but the wheels have already been set in motion. This has created the snowball effect in the gap of sexual morals between men and women and we have reached the point of no return. But because of what our world was founded upon and because of what was passed down, we live in that same moral pattern. In this day and time, it is still seen as much worse for a woman to be promiscuous versus a man.

Let's look at the symbolization of a woman's body in a deeper way. The Bible tells us that the woman was made from man, so in a way she belonged to the man, one man. Although a woman was one of a thousand wives, she was only for that man. Traditionally, women have been groomed and trained to be a man's wife all their lives. Women married and bore children at early ages. Because there were so many more women than men, one man could be with many women sexually because it was normal and a part of life. Men knew the structure of the world when it came to reproduction of mankind. It was no mystery or secret that men slept with many different women. If it were ever the other way around, a woman did it because she was cast out and needed the money. Even in the days of the Bible there were women who were called harlots. In this day and time we call the harlot a prostitute or whore. Back then it only took one man to impregnate a woman, and after that, that man became the only man whose children she was expected to bear. This idea has continued, even into present day.

Diving deeper into the *history* discussion, I will now focus on how we are what we were made of. Although we have laws that prevent us from having more than one wife or cheating on our mate, moral standards are in place that convict promiscuity. Granted, these times are not the same as those of old. And our history has been deeply ingrained in the way we govern our bodies and our actions. Regardless, the same rules we were created to live by still govern our hearts today, whether we like it or not. As a people, we are what we are, and as men, we are completely different from women when it comes to the ways of the heart, which determines the morals that we collectively decide to live by. The reason is a man was not created the same as a woman, and our gender roles are different. We are not made the same; our feelings and our emotions are quite opposite. Men were made to hunt and to fight and to kill. Thus, our hearts are not easily tied to one thing because at any given time we might have to forfeit that one thing we love the most. On the other hand, in the days of old a woman was made to serve her man and be almost like a footstool. A woman did not go out to battle. She stayed back and kept the house and the children in order. A woman did not make decisions or call any shots. Because of this difference in our social roles, our morals about sex are completely the opposite. A woman was a prize for a man after he had won a battle in a war or a duel against another man. A man was never a gift to a woman, and that man could not be replaced with another man – but in an instant that woman could be replaced.

Therefore, it is of the utmost importance for a woman to understand the makeup of a man and the history (his-story) plus the biography of mankind, to understand why there has always been a double standard when it comes to sex. Although women are empowered in this day and age, the fact that society never conditioned us to be seen as equals will always leave the scales tipped to one side when it comes to sexual morality. Ask yourself this question: "Do I want to be able to sleep with as many men as I can before I die to feel more like a woman?" I can almost guarantee that the majority of you answer, "No." In fact, the fewer men you sleep with, the more you feel like a woman. But some, if not most men, will ask themselves, "Do I want to be able to sleep with as many women as I can before I die?" and I can guarantee the majority of them will say "Yes" to that question. This simple question suggests that men and women do not view the world through the same lens, so, in many cases, what we hold sacred in our hearts and minds is often completely different.

To sum it all up, the Bible says a woman was made from the rib of a man and therefore she is called woMAN. One woman belongs to one man but it is perceived that one man could belong to many women. It is not conceivably possible for a woman to have two husbands in any land; and even in most religions it is not condoned. Actually it is not condoned for a man to have more than one woman in many different regions of the world. Religions inside of those regions still believe that it is OK, and who is to blame them for continuing in the way that the world was began? Since this is what was set in motion since the beginning of time, you have the double standard between men and women regarding to sex. Now I ask you: "Do you want to sleep with as many men as you can?" or "Do you want men to sleep with a few women?"

CHAPTER 5

Does a "Beautiful Woman" Stop a Man From Cheating?

1 Peter 3:3-4 – "Your beauty should not come from outward adornment, such as braided hair and the wearing of gold jewelry and fine clothes instead it should be that of your inner self, the unfading beauty of a gentle and quiet spirit, which is of great worth in Gods sight."

Beauty alone cannot stop a man from cheating! Cheating is a decision, not an uncontrollable behavior. The beauty of a woman would have to be inside and out, and flawless in order for a man to stop cheating. In other words, a woman with insecurities would fall from the category of "perfect beauty."

There is no such thing as an

unattractive woman, and to understand why beauty can't stop a man from cheating, you must understand what constitutes beauty in the mind of a man. Before you get confused, I want to explain that, when I say unattractive, I don't mean ugly, I mean less attractive. For example, Beyonce is what I consider attractive and Macy Gray would be less attractive, not ugly just less attractive. Beauty is in the eye of the beholder.

An unattractive woman may have more of a chance of having a faithful man than an attractive woman. The reason is because an unattractive woman lacks *runway or natural beauty*, so she must compensate for that in other ways like a beautiful personality, a meek spirit, a passionate heart, and a submissive will. Those qualities are not taught; they are learned along the way in life. A woman either has them or she doesn't. The qualities that most unattractive women share are the qualities that speak to the heart of a man and not to his sexual drive. Those qualities are what causes him to be faithful. This unattractive woman grabs a man in a much deeper way than a woman with a beautiful face. This woman goes well beneath the surface of his rough exterior and grabs what is most dear to him. You see, an unattractive woman will unknowingly make a man feel like a King just because of the qualities she has picked up along the way. This sense of control and manliness means so much more to a man than a pretty face. The feeling an unattractive woman may give a man can never be replaced because it is familiar and comforting. When I say comforting, I mean back to the beginning of time when a man was King and woman was Queen. To the times when she was the heart and he was the head. This is where a man feels at home because, according to the Bible, this is how God created a man to exist. A man may meet an unattractive woman and become friends just to get a better idea on the female perspective of life, and before you know it, he could fall in love. It is true that when finding love with the heart, opposites attract. It's hard for a man to fall in love with an unattractive woman because her lack of beauty may put up an extra barrier that he has to break through; but it's even harder to leave her alone after he's fallen for her. There's something about her qualities that lets him rest at ease. But, it's sad to say, when a man leaves an unattractive woman, nine out of ten times it's for a more attractive woman.

The different qualities in an attractive woman can be found and understood very easily. Let me break it down. She is beautiful, so she gets doors opened and held for her; she doesn't have to hold them herself. She is beautiful, so she gets extra gifts on birthdays and holidays. She is beautiful, so she gets extra food in the drive thru at McDonalds or she gets to skip the line at the club while the less attractive women wait in the cold. Now, the beautiful woman expects to be given free food, she expects to be skipped ahead in line, and for the door to be held. Then, when she is in a relationship, because she is beautiful, every man she dates feels he has to impress her or put her on a pedestal. As he pushes her up, all she can do is to look down upon him. This gives her a certain attitude that doesn't allow her to be submissive like she was as a little girl. Now she wants her way and she expects nothing less. This beautiful girl is slowly becoming a monster on the inside, and the only time she is genuine is when she is alone. Over the years, her kindness and humility is scraped away and replaced with arrogance and a selfish spirit. What this beautiful girl doesn't realize is that her man hates almost every part of her but he can't overpower her beauty. She doesn't realize that he enjoys being away from her to get a break. The only time he is truly happy is when she is quiet and they are walking and all the other men are lusting after what he has. This beautiful woman has filled her head up to believe that she is beautiful all the way through and can't see that she has no plausible qualities as a woman.

All that goes into play when a man cheats on a woman. There's more. There is something I like to call the "one flaw rule." The rule states that if there is one thing wrong with you, then that gives your man the room he needs to cheat. I know it's hard to swallow. You're saying to yourself, "How unfair, no one is perfect". And you're very right; but such is life. You see, a man will sleep with a woman for one thing that he likes about her. You may be beautiful, but he hates the fact that you can't cook, so he cheats with a woman who can. You may be beautiful, but you have dark brown eyes, so he cheats with a woman with light brown eyes. You may be beautiful, but you don't have the smallest waist with a big butt, so he cheats with a woman who does. Are you getting the picture? A man may sleep with this other woman because she has green eyes, then he'll sleep with this other woman because she has sexy thighs. Then he may sleep with one because she can sing, and one because she has a degree, or one because she drives a nice car. All it takes is one thing that he sees/likes, and that will draw him in. That goes back to why a King would have so many wives; it only makes sense. Each woman is unique in her own way, and no two are the same. Think about the possibilities a man has when choosing women. There is an endless supply. Because you're beautiful doesn't mean a thing since there is always someone else who has something you don't, and that's what keeps this vicious cycle going. Understand, unless you're perfect in every single way shape or form, there is a possibility your man is going to cheat; and if he is fly enough to get you, then I can almost guarantee he'll want to pursue another one.

That ties right into the confidence theory. When a man can get a pretty woman it gives him all the confidence in the world. Just like in anything you do, if you do it once you feel like you can do it again. Don't feel like, "Oh, he has me, and I'm prettier than all these other girls, so he won't want anyone else". That's the last thing that should cross your mind. Remember, curiosity killed the cat. When a man gets one beautiful lady, he automatically wonders if he can get another. Some pretty girls who have been cheated on say, "I'm going to get a fat black guy who will never cheat on me because he appreciates my beauty."

I witnessed a funny story when it comes to this. My sister once met a guy over the phone. She hadn't met him in person but they were talking for months every single day. She grew to love him because he was so nice and so funny. He would treat her like a Queen; he would talk and laugh with her for hours on end. She felt like she was on top of the world because she finally found a man who respected her and treated her like she deserved to be treated. One day they finally met; he was about 6'5", and he weighed about 140 pounds. He was like a tall stick. He had on a very dingy outfit, and he was very less fortunate. He had a huge birthmark in the middle of his face that killed any chance of him being attractive. Now, my sister was beautiful. She was about 5'4", 115 pounds. She had hair that came to the middle of her back, and she had a perfect smile and a beautiful face. Because she had already fallen in love she couldn't tell how ugly he was. All she saw was a person who treated her like a Queen. I will never forget him because he took her virginity and changed the way I saw guys like him. They dated for a while, I'd say about a year or longer. Throughout most of the relationship, he was Prince Charming but towards the one-year mark things began to change. He was beginning to get used to this beautiful girl, and he loved her as arm candy. He had taken her most prized possession and shelved it as his trophy. What happened is this chump had found his swagger with my sister. She gave him a profound confidence that radiated like the sun. All of a sudden, this ugly duck was the big swan of the pond. He began to attract other very beautiful women because they were wondering what was it about him that my sister wanted. The other girls were drawn to this swagger. It changed his life, he got a job so he could dress better and he even practiced harder so he could start on his varsity team, on which he had ridden the bench prior to meeting my sister.

Now, you have this very unattractive guy who had found himself through this beautiful girl, and all of a sudden he was Morris Chestnut. He began to cheat on my sister with the other beautiful girls that were drawn to him. He started yelling and cursing my sister just like the handsome jocks use to, and now he was just another guy. I shared my story to emphasize how I formed my *confidence theory*, and since then I've seen it over and over again.

Besides the *one flaw rule* and the *confidence theory*, you have the almost impossible task of finding a completely beautiful woman. For example, you have the rich beautiful woman and the poor beautiful woman. I use rich and poor in the same sense as attractive and unattractive. I'm not saying there isn't a middle. I'm just using the extremes so the examples can better illustrate my point. The rich beautiful girl is catered to hand-and-foot and is brought up to expect that. She is arrogant and rude. She expects the finer things in life and will settle for nothing less. That's why they end up NFL or NBA wives. They will deal with the cheating and the beating as long as they can rock the Prada and Gucci. Rich beauty may date cute, but most likely they will marry rich. If you are this woman, this may sit right in your lap. So ask yourself these questions: "Can I cook? Do I like to clean? Do I yell back at him when he yells at me? Do I curse at him? Do I ignore what he tells me to do and do exactly what I want? Be honest with yourself, nobody is listening but you. Now, if you answered "Yes" to all of those questions or all but one or two, that's why your beauty won't stop him from cheating!

Then you have the poor and beautiful. This is a touchy case because most of these women have had so few resources or been through so much they still have trouble sleeping at night. Although most of the things they've experienced are not their fault, they suffer the consequences just as if they chose to be poor and beautiful. Most of the poor and beautiful women I've encountered had no father figure or positive role models. They were from single parent homes where they couldn't be fully trained how to be a classy lady. A lot of these women moved from place to place, and the mother worked two and three jobs, often nights. These beautiful ladies were left to the wolves that we call *men*. These men would rape and molest these very young, innocent, and beautiful girls.. These girls were without protection or anyone to turn to, so this is what they had to accept. This scarred them for life and eventually affected the way they interacted with men in their adult lives. Many were lost along the way and got caught up in sex at a young age, and those that engage in sex willingly still suffered because they, too, were possibly raped. If you are this girl, ask yourself these questions. "Was I molested at a young age? Was I brainwashed by older boys at a young age? Did I give in to sex because I thought it was expected of me? Did I get pregnant before my 18th birthday? Did I get raped before my 18th birthday? Have I stripped or had sex for money?" If you answered "Yes" to all of these questions or to all but one or two, my heart goes out to you. This is why your beauty won't stop your man from cheating on you. Even though what happened to you is not your fault, it still hurts that man in your life to know you've been with men. Because of that he has no sense of ownership, so he searches for it with other women on the side.

In this chapter I have shared reasons why I believe beauty can't stop a man from cheating and the reasons why it's almost impossible for a woman to have it all. All of us are shaped by our experiences. That's why Queens aren't humble as servants and servants aren't arrogant as Queens. All women are beautiful, regardless of what standard or measure is used, and every man must recognize that to be true. Your beauty is what it is and that's what it has made you and because no beauty can be perfect, your beauty alone can't keep a man faithful.

CHAPTER 6

Why Is It So Easy For Some Guys to End a Relationship?

Contrary to popular belief a man takes a break up harder than a woman, even if the man is the one who initiates the break up. The fact that men don't openly show their emotions makes dealing with things a lot harder than it does for women. A woman can break down and cry anywhere, and it's accepted. That means whenever she's hurting she can just cry it out, no matter where she is or what she is doing, and that's OK. On the other hand, a man has to do it in his closet or when he is all alone. That makes it harder for a man to get over his problems. Whereas a woman can cry all day everywhere she goes, a man has to save his tears until he gets home. It may seem like that man is not disturbed, but on the inside he is torn apart when his emotional balance is challenged. This chapter covers the *upgrade* rule and my theory that the only way to forget something old is to replace it with something new.

When a man has a woman, he is only focused on her until he gets to know her. For every man it takes a different amount of time, meaning that for one man it may be six months, and for the next man a year, and the next man five years. Regardless of the amount of time, that becomes all the time you get from that man. After a man is used to you – and you are very predictable to him and the sex is boring and nothing exciting is happening – then he starts looking for your replacement. Finding a replacement could take years. So, you can be with a man five or ten years thinking that he is in it for the long run, but the reality is he hasn't been able to find someone else who intrigues him more than you did. Instead of just being alone, he stays with you so he can still have a partner, regular sex, and so forth. No one wants to be alone and miserable, not even a man. It's sad because he is plotting his escape, and you have no idea of what is happening.

Understand that while you are with your man, he is looking around trying to find the next woman he can get to know. He will venture into the lives of many different women looking to see if each has something you don't. This won't be something sexual, it gets deeper than that. For example, you may be in college and studying to be a lawyer or a doctor. You also have your own car, and you live in college apartments. On top of all that you are a decent looking person. Then one day he meets a girl who is studying to be a doctor also, but her car is a little nicer than yours, her rent is a little higher than yours, and she is just as pretty. That makes that woman an upgrade from you. This is what can take his interest away from you and compel him to move on. While he's getting to know her, he could be getting ready to make his transition from you to her. All of a sudden, for example, he realizes she isn't as clean and neat as you, so he lets her go and puts his focus back on you. Now he's appreciating your cleanliness a little more than he did before because he's had something to compare it to. Later, he could meet a woman who is studying to be a lawyer. She has a car, her own place, and she's prettier than you. Then, once again, he is getting ready to make his transition from you to her. All of a sudden, as another example, he realizes that she is bull-headed and stubborn, while you are humble and submissive. He then lets her go and comes back to you, appreciating your humility more than ever. Understand that he keeps pulling away and then comes back stronger and seemingly so much more in love. This keeps you on an emotional roller coaster, but at the same time is intriguing to you and keeps you on your toes. You're playing right into his trap! You love him like never before because he keeps coming out of the blue, loving you like crazy, and putting you on cloud nine. All the while, your relationship isn't fazing him at all. He just has to adjust and give you another brownie point for being more unique than the next woman. All he has to do is just keep looking. He could go through a hundred women before he finds one that is better than you all the way around. Then and only then is when he'll leave. He won't leave you for someone that isn't as good as you, which would be stupid of him. This is why I call it an upgrade. To this type of man, you're just like a car or his clothes. After a while, they get old, and you have to upgrade to something bigger and better to feel fresh again.

My mother told me to never speak numbers in regards to my love life, but if I didn't, I wouldn't be completely honest. I would be just like every other man you've met, and the point of this book is to be just the opposite. Once I was with a woman, and it took me about two months to get used to her. Then we had to go home for the summer, and with her not being there I couldn't hold out on my life. I wasn't sure we'd work out, so I kept looking. In the meantime, she got my name tattooed on her, but I was in the process of looking for a new girlfriend. Then we went back to school, and she said she had to make a confession. She made me promise that I wouldn't get mad and that I would get over it as soon as she told me. I promised that. She then admitted to going to a movie with a male friend of her sister, as well as going to a party where her ex-boyfriend was in attendance. I thought to myself, "Are you serious?" She had to take deep breaths and everything before she told me. Then I said, "OK, well I have some confessions, too." I gave her the same stipulations that she had given me. Then I told her that I had been with nine different women in that three month hiatus. She just swallowed deep, and we brushed it off. Of course, later it hit her very hard and she released the emotions she had held back at the moment I told her. She stayed with me, though, and that made me love her even more. It wasn't good enough to have a woman who would stay with me after relationships with nine other girls. I got involved with another one that semester and then went home for Christmas break and continued with two or three more women. Then, I went back to school and cheated with another. That next summer, my girlfriend came home and stayed with me to keep a close eye on me. Although she lived with me, I still managed to sleep with another girl twice right under her nose. Then we went to different schools the next fall, and I went with six more girls. After all that, I still hadn't found an upgrade. Understand I hadn't confessed since I confessed to the first nine, so she was deep in love, and somewhat happy. She still continued to be upset and worried about the nine other women and had no clue it was actually more than that! To make a long story short, I went through 26 other women before I found my upgrade. I'll have you know that number is about average for most of my peers. I was with her for two years and in those two years it took me 26 experiments before I found the right upgrade. When I found my upgrade, I just called her and told her it was over and moved on with my life. I ended up going back to her for a few months when my upgrade and I had our problems. She fell in love all over again, and then my upgrade and I reconnected, hit it off again, and I called my fiancée and told her it was over for the second time, and that time it was for real.

As a woman, I don't want you to think that I'm one in a million. I am just like most of the other men I've ever met when it comes to women. I've done a lot, and what I haven't done I've seen the rest. It's probably safe to say your man is just like me, and, right now while you're reading this, if he's not beside you reading along he could be looking for his upgrade. Don't be naïve and think you are better than any other woman around you and that he'll have to look a million years before he finds his upgrade. Please don't get complacent and think that just because you have his child, live in his house, or drive a car under his name that he won't up and leave without warning. Many marriages end after

20 or more years. You may even know someone personally who has gone through what I've described. Oftentimes, the man decides to move on.

So you see, what makes it so easy for a man to leave a relationship is his upgrade. In order to forget something old, you must replace it with something new; this is what every man knows. Otherwise, you'd end up going back to that same old fling. A man bides his time watching and waiting for the woman that will sweep him off his feet and give him the strength he needs to move on. When I left my fiancée, I thought about her for nights on end, but as long as my upgrade was on her game and keeping me interested I couldn't allow myself to move backwards. The reason a man leaves you so easily is that he has other options, while you are saying to yourself "He doesn't even care." Please believe that he cares probably more than you do, but the reason you can't see it is that his time is being occupied elsewhere. I can assure you that every waking moment his upgrade isn't by his side you're the only thing on his mind and he has to fight himself not to call you and make up. You can be sure that if he does leave with ease, and then all of a sudden he's back knocking on your door, it's because his upgrade turned out to be a downgrade – but it took him a while to figure it out.

Please know that it has nothing to do with you as a woman when a man leaves you and doesn't look back. It's what he's found that is keeping him occupied and satisfied. With that said, condition your heart to run the long race and endure to the end. Every relationship has ups and downs, and the majority of the time it is due to the other woman in his life. If your man gets up and leaves you with no remorse while you sit and cry your eyes out day after day, and then one day he comes back, remember what you read here today. Remember that, just like he left you with ease one time, he can do so even easier a second time. It may take years, and that's what some women let fool them. If you look around, you'll find many women who had a man take 20 or more years before he found his upgrade. Very rarely do you hear of the woman leaving the man. Your man could have a stroke or a heart attack and become a paraplegic and you still stay with him. If the shoe was on the other foot, you could end up very lonely. I'm not saying freeze your heart and shut your man out. I'm saying condition your heart for the worse and hope for the best.

Just like with every problem, there are some possible solutions. From a man that has up and left you without even leaving a note, my advice would be to stay unpredictable. Just like you've read in other chapters, I encourage you to stay one step ahead of the game. Don't allow yourself to go into a lull and let your love life lose its flame. Study your man, know what he likes, and always think outside of the box. You have to set yourself up to a point that a woman would have to go to the moon and back to sweep your man off his feet. If other women are wearing boots, then you wear tennis shoes. If the fling you found out about has extensions, then extend yours longer and put curls in it. If she shops at Body Shop, then you go to Express, do what you have to do to keep the edge. For example, most men drink, smoke, or curse, knowing that I do none of the three. Most men hide their feelings, so, knowing that, I write poetry. Most men have too much pride to cater to their woman; knowing that, I cook my wife breakfast and get her unexpected flowers and jewelry. This ensures that in order for her to find a man better than me she will have to search the entire globe to do so. Thus, in order to prevent your man from leaving you without a warning or walking out and never looking back, set yourself apart. Don't feel like this is too much for love; true love is worth it. Go above and beyond the call of love and do things that you know other women won't do. The quote for my senior class in high school was "Do today what others won't, so tomorrow you can do what others can't." That quote means so much and can take you so far in so many different aspects of life.

CHAPTER 7

Why do Some Men Physically (hit) Abuse Women?

There could be many reasons why a man is compelled to strike or physically abuse a woman, and for many men the reasons are the same. I will touch on what I believe are primary reasons for this cruel and sad circumstance. As a woman, you should never blame yourself or feel like you deserve to be beaten. There is absolutely nothing that gives a man the right to physically or emotionally harm you. I don't believe a man should ever be an enforcer in a relationship. No relationship is going to be successful by force.

One reason some men beat women is that they saw this happen between their father and mother when they were growing up. As a young man, you look up to your father, and everything you see him do is instilled in you. Sometimes men become the same men their fathers were, even though they may not want to. If a man watches his father become physical with his mother in order to gain respect or run his house, then that boy will grow up and run his home the same way. We are all puppets on a string, and we only do what we have seen someone else do. Therefore, for many men their father is the reason they beat on the women in their lives.

Another reason is the life that man has led. If a man was a submissive and passive child and teenager, then he took a lot of stuff that a man is not used to taking. There are many boys that you knew who would get jumped or beat up at school. Or maybe they were in the "In Crowd," but they weren't seen as the tough guy. They could have been the pretty boy or the rich guy so that made them cool. Naturally, that man was "soft" as a young boy and as a teen did everything in his power to avoid confrontations with other men. Either he was terrified by the brutality of fights or physical sports, or he felt weak and inferior to other guys his age. For this reason, that young man concealed his feelings, especially his hatred because he was the lesser of his peers. He had no one he could look down on or overpower. So, when he was enraged it had to be suppressed because there was nothing he could do about it. This same young man may have bullied his female siblings if he had any, or his younger family members so he could feel powerful in some way. Here is a scenario to consider. If you put a can of sweet smelling air freshener in a hot shed outside, and everyday it gets hotter and hotter, one day it is going to explode. The same happens with that young man. He is soft to begin with, and on top of that he is forced to suppress his feelings of anger and rage every time something bad happens. One day when he is eventually able to overpower someone, he will do just that. This is what forms an abusive man. As you may have learned in a class or two, people are products of their environments. Men who suffered that form of abuse will grow to be abusers.

I can speak from experience because I was once that little boy. I was raised with a mother and a father, so I didn't have to struggle. Without that struggle, I wasn't forced to become tough and fend for my own. I was very well taken care of. I was from a quiet home and was raised to be meek and humble. Hence I didn't speak up for myself, nor did I want to fight for what was mine. Many times I walked away from fights and bottled my anger. When I did fight I never lost a fight, but that was because I released on that person all the emotional anger I had held in for so long. I rarely fought because I didn't like the brutality of it. Therefore, my experience has helped me hone in on this subject. I grew up to be an abusive man with one of my counterparts. I had held within me so many frustrations for so many years, that when I finally was the bigger and more powerful of the two, I took advantage of it. As sad as it is to say, and as much of a shock it may be for those who know me, I am man enough to admit it. In order for a man to come out of it, he must first be able to admit it. I know a lot of men just like me, but they are afraid to admit that they, too, let their own self-hate get the best of them. My testimony is that I came out of it. A man doesn't grow out of it, he has to face himself in the mirror and confront himself so that he can become a real man. I decided to let that relationship go and turned over a new leaf and become brand new again. This time I am living my life as a real man, a man who is too much of a man to hit someone weaker than himself.

As I said, I had to come out of that relationship because inside of it I could have never changed. It was something in her spirit that didn't connect with mine. No matter how delicate it was, it would trigger a rage inside of me that turned me into a beast. That is why I feel the need to warn every woman who reads this book and is in an abusive relationship: the only way for the abuse or the pain to stop is for you to come out of it. Once a man has a connection to abusing you, then that's the only way he can express himself when he is angry unless he just stops caring at all. If you are in an abusive relationship, you can probably recall when it started as just a push. Next, it was a choke. Then, it was a push and a choke. Later, it turned into slaps and punches or body slams of some sort. Just like any negative behavior that isn't stopped, it only gets worse. I tell every woman I know who is in an abusive relationship to get out because no matter how long it takes, one day it'll result in death. A man will continue to escalate and go one step further each time. I watched it happen in me, and I've watched it happen in the relationships of my loved ones. I know women with permanent swollen lips and eyes because of abusive relationships. I have aunts with deformed body parts because of broken bones that were never fixed. They came out of that relationship, and that is the only reason why they are alive today. Domestic violence is very serious and should never be taken lightly. I thank God for delivering me from the vice grip the devil had on my life. Now, my wife can vouch for me and say that I am a real man who handles my problems like a man. I am no longer afraid to confront myself or my problems like a man. It isn't a matter of a man being afraid of other men. Now, it's a matter of that man being afraid of himself. He knows there is something defective inside of him, whereas if he goes off, he could annihilate whatever is in his path without even blinking. That is why he must be able to confront himself.

As a woman, you have to know your man. Communication is the key. Engage in conversations that will answer the questions you need to know about his personality. If he is a no-nonsense person, then take him at his word, value and respect that. As a woman, you have to understand that a man lives by his pride and his pride alone. If you are with a man that is not naturally abusive and shows no signs of why he should be, there is still a possibility that you can be abused. There are some ways you can avoid it, though. Start by being able to communicate effectively. Respond to your man in a way that shows your concern and love for him. Be open to communicate with him and listen to what he has to say. Make sure he understands that you want to be heard, too. It is hard for a man to hit anything that looks helpless. If you are listening to him and you are making direct eye contact, hitting you will not be an option. Sometimes a confrontation between a couple is escalated unnecessarily. If he yells and you yell right back, you challenge him as a man. If he is talking and you talk over him, you challenge him as a man. If he moves to escape and you step in front of him, you challenge him as a man. If he curses at you and you curse back at him, you challenge him as a man. The male persona is unique. Some men see disagreements with their mates as a challenge or confrontation. You must follow certain rules of engagement in all settings. It's important that you remember how a man thinks and operates, and if you can't respect him as a man then you shouldn't be with him. If you provoke a man to hit you just like another man does, then he'll hit you just like he'd hit another man. Respect his manhood, as you expect him to respect your womanhood. That way, if he is not naturally abusive, you won't have to worry about him becoming that way.

Now, if you read this and you can honestly say you do all those things correctly and that you give your man no reason to go any further than a conversation, but he still abuses you, then it's time for you to leave. If a man can't solve a problem with you by talking it out, then you shouldn't be with him. If a man jumps to conclusions without hearing you out and taking you at your word, then you shouldn't be with him. Any man who has to resolve a problem with a woman through physical abuse is not a real man, and deep down he knows it. The best thing you can do for him is leave. Many women condone abusive behavior by accepting it and reinforcing it. When I was in an abusive relationship, my counterpart would reward my abuse with sex. Therefore I would have never come out of that stage of my life if I had left it up to her. If she had ignored me after that or started distancing herself from me, then it would have brought me back to my senses much faster. If your other half is abusive, show him you don't appreciate it by distancing yourself from him. Cut off your love and communication with him. It'll either cause him to become more violent or change because he knows he is losing you. The sad thing is, if you go back, then eventually he'll go back to the same abusive man he was before. Then you are forced to leave him. Remember, any man who truly loves you will never lay a hand on you!

CHAPTER 8

Why do Some Black Men Choose White Women?

This is a very intriguing question, and a lot of women have inquired about it. There isn't any one answer to this question, and each man will have his own personal reason. I can speak for myself on this question, because there was a period in my life when I ventured this way. I believe my reasons are similar to other black men who've dated white women.

Let me begin by distinguishing black women and white women as their own separate entities. Black women and white women are very different from each other. Just like many questions the answers to why black men cross the racial divide in dating lie in history, and in this case so does the difference in black and white women. Let's look back into the days of slavery in America: you have the black woman who was a servant to her white master, and the white woman who was a servant to her white master. The catch is that they served in two very different ways, and this shaped these two women quite differently. A black woman was forced to pick cotton in the heat of the day right next to her man with her kids trailing behind. This black woman had to be just as strong as her male counterpart. She was expected to perform the same duties with no exceptions. Because of this, black women were built tough and forced to stand on their own two feet. At any moment, their other half could be sold to another master or killed as punishment by his master. The black woman had to weather the storm and be able to stand regardless. A black woman was made a strong individual by the things she suffered and she would pass that same strength and integrity on to her daughters and granddaughters. This is how we got strong independent black women in the 21st Century. I do believe that over the years black women have taken this strength and integrity and lost its essence. Now it is a proud spirit that ends in a fall. A black woman prides herself on having her own job, her own car, and her own place to live. A black woman is proud to say, "I don't mind having a man, but I don't need a man." Truthfully, she is a product of her ancestors, who toiled in the hot beating sun and worked their fingers to the bone right beside their man, while still respecting him as a man. Now, we have very independent black women.

On the other hand, you have the white woman, who was also a servant, but she was married to the master. The white woman was there to aid her master in whatever way she needed to, while knowing he was sleeping with the black slave women. She stood by him and took care of her children. The white women were there to cook breakfast, lunch, and dinner, or order the black maid to do so. As a white woman, she was free of physical labor, and the stress that came with it. A white woman was the helper to her man. Her duties were to clean the house and make sure the kids were well fed and cleaned daily. The white mother would teach her daughter how to cook and clean for her man and show her, by example, how to listen and respect a man. The white mother brought her daughter up to cater to her man in order to ensure a wealthy and established life style. She also was taught that black men were forbidden fruit and never to be touched. Think of this as an analogy liking unto Eve and the forbidden fruit. There is some truth to the notion that as humans we want what we can't have. Because of the long tradition in white culture today, there are still many obedient, submissive– but oftentimes secretly deviant – white women. What has changed, however, is that women aren't bound by color barriers anymore, and it is fair to say they can eat the fruit of any tree they please.

In my opinion, that is the difference between black and white women. And the history of black and white women has enabled me to understand who they are today. The reasons a black man goes white are almost obvious in some ways. The least of the reasons would be revenge. As a black man, we often feel as if we are held down by the white man. In order to surpass them in America, we have to be twice as good. Not every black man wants to rap or play sports, but those are the areas white men say we can have. Some black men want to be doctors and lawyers or best-selling authors. In America, those are viewed as white men's jobs because they require a good education, and, because of slavery, many black men are behind the learning curve. Some black men may want what a white man has in some areas of his life. If he can't get that, then he'll settle for his women instead. Every black man knows there is nothing a white man hates more than seeing a black man with a white woman. If that's a man's reason, then it has nothing to do with a black woman. In essence, that black man has nothing against his own kind. He's just caught up fighting his battle against the white man with the wrong weapon, the white woman!

Another reason black men go white is to see what it's like. Generally speaking, I've learned through my studies that men are not racist towards women. In other words, virtually, any color man, black, white, or otherwise, will sleep with a woman of any color. To a man, sex is sex, and there isn't much difference between the races. Some black men are curious as to whether the grass is greener on the other side of the fence; so, they jump the fence with no intentions of staying, only sometimes they get trapped on that side. I believe the men who do it as an experiment plan to return and marry their own. They just want to see what it feels like. If you recall what I discussed in previous chapters, a man is from descendants who were able to have hundreds of wives and concubines of all different races and colors. So as with men crossing the racial divide, like any experiment, you test until you are able to prove your hypothesis. That is, some men discover that white women are of little difference and they move on.

Lastly, I feel the main reason a black man goes for white females is due to the differences between the two races. Some black men have controlling personalities, and many black women aren't going to put up with this type of persosnality unless she was raised like a white woman. I've dated that type of black woman, too. Indeed, that was very interesting, but that's a whole different story that I won't address in this book! Many black men want to feel like a King after a long day's work, but, as in the days of slavery, the 21st century woman has probably worked just as hard. My mother was famous for this line: "I work just like you do!" My father would be frustrated and tired because he'd worked in the hot sun all day – and my mother worked in a place that was air-conditioned – and justifiably, wouldn't cook or clean when she came home.

On the other hand, consider the white household, where many white mothers don't have to work. Typically, these women are called housewives. They live just like they did in the days of slavery and their only job is to cater to their men. When a black man ventures toward a white woman, he is likely going from a black woman who responds, "Your hands and legs ain't broke – you clean it! " when he asks her to clean up. He leaves his black woman for a white woman who says, "Yeah, I'll clean it, no problem." To hear that response is much m ore appealing, and in his mind, makes him feel "so much more like a man." In a way, we automatically go back to when we were Kings.

So much more evidence can be presented to show why some black men prefer white women. In fact, there are countless scenarios in which these two women will react differently. The reality is that the majority of men who cross this line are in favor of the white woman. A white woman will go where you tell her to go and do what you tell her to do with no questions asked. For your birthday and Christmas, she showers you with gifts and makes you feel like a King. Many black women I've met would rather receive than give, and, when they do give, they won't go broke doing so. White women will. When a black woman receives, she almost expects her man to go beyond her expectations. White women are intimidated by black men because they know the stock we are made from. They come to a black man to find a sense of security that she couldn't find with a white man; therefore, she serves that man happily. Black women are not intimidated by black men at all. This is because she comes from a line of women that had to do the same work a man did. I'm sure you've seen a black female swear up and down she will fight a man and bluff as if she can physically keep up with him in a fight. It's funny when you think about it. White women won't even test it because they already are in fear of that man. These differences are why black men go white and end up staying on that side of the fence. It may be sad to a black woman, but it's true.

When you see an NBA player or a doctor and lawyer go to a white woman, just know it's because he feels black women are too much of a headache for his career. He would rather come home and be the boss after a long hard day than have to come home to fight for territory and declare his manhood in his own home. So the reason is not because he wants to give more to someone that already has the world, as I've heard many black women say. It's simply because of the difference in the way the women react to their man. Some black men are not strong enough or built to share their throne or split the jeans so that both can wear a pair. They'd rather be the head and have a tail than have two heads on the same body.

As a black woman, in order to prevent this from happening to you there are some changes you would have to make. I'll have you know I came back to my own; I have a beautiful black Queen who realizes there is no room for pride in love. She made the changes many black women need to make to avoid ending up single or watching her man leave for a white woman. As a black woman, you have to realize that it is OK to have a man take care of you. It's OK to listen and let a man lead if you know he loves and respects you. If he loves you, then put your heart in his hands and trust, as well as expect him not to break it. As written in the Bible, God created a man to lead. If you are a woman and you have a man, you should expect him to "man up" in hard times.

When all is going wrong and you don't know what you are going to do next, tradition has it that you turn to him and lean on him for his strength. If you can do that in a time of need, then you will likely be able to do that when times are good also. It's not fair to a man when you cater to him as soon as you need rent or a car note paid.

I've asked my wife to let me lead our household, and entrust me to lead this relationship in a righteous and spiritual way. I told her that I would love her whether we were up or down and, and no matter what. I would be the man of our household. At some point in the maturation and spiritual growth of our marriage, she realized that I really do love her and she gave me her load to carry. I bear that every day with pride, knowing that no matter what I say my wife will listen and be open to communicating with me no matter what. There is no greater feeling than for a man to feel like he is *the man*, especially in his own castle, with a loving and understanding mate. I encourage you to be open to communicating with your man and not strip him of his pride and sense of manhood. That is the only thing God gave a man that he can't live without. If you know that man loves you with all of his heart and you feel that he wouldn't do anything to hurt you, then love and let go of your pride. We are not slaves any more and you don't have to work as hard as your man. The world is changing and allowing black men to be just as wealthy as white men. If you want to be that man's woman instead of seeing another good brother go white, then it's up to you.

I will end this chapter with a quote from the Bible. This comes from I Corinthians 13:4-8 and it reads, *"Love suffers long and is kind; love does not envy: love does not parade itself, is not puffed up; Does not behave rudely, does not seek its own, is not provoked, thinks no evil; Does not rejoice in iniquity, but rejoices in the truth; Bears all things, hopes all things, endures all things. Love never fails"*.

CHAPTER 9

Why Is It That Some Men Cheat With Less Attractive Women?

This is a funny but worthy question. The answer is simple, though: when your man cheats with a woman who isn't as pretty as you, it's because he's not looking to replace you, he's just trying to sew his wild oats. To begin, I'll touch on the difference between flings and the reason a man has flings. Everything about this answer is important and vital to your understanding a man's thought process behind cheating.

First, you have the cute fling. This woman is the one your man can see himself being with, so he takes his time with her. This is the woman whom he will call his friend or his homie. This is the woman whom he will spend quality time with, whether it is in person or on the phone. This is the woman you will likely accept because, if not, he'll just leave you and focus on her-- and he almost makes it clear to you that this will be the case. This woman is probably the *friend*, that you know about but haven't seen, nor does he want you to see. He emphasizes that they are just friends, and that's that. She knows all about you and is cool with your man just being her friend, although she may like him. In a way, she counts on him to make all the moves – if any – therefore, she doesn't have to get beat up for trying your man. This woman most likely has a life of her own because a cute fling won't wait around on a man and is usually in a relationship already and is just trying new things for a while. This is the female that you don't have to worry about anything physical happening between them; because when that happens you can be certain he'll soon leave you. When he knows it's time for that, you and he will most likely take a "break" or just break up. He may plan to come back to you after he gets what he wants from the cute fling; she doesn't know that, but she won't do anything sexually with him until he is rid of you. That way, she doesn't have to worry about feeling like she is second string. Cute flings are sometimes demanding, so it's either just friends or they want it all, nothing in between. So, here we are not talking about "friends with benefits". There will only be emotional cheating with this woman. This is the worst type of fling because this fling can actually ruin your relationship without your even knowing it's happening. This usually happens all of a sudden, with no indications before it does. You even overlook many arguments that you brush off as normal relationship drama. When he's gone, it doesn't mean he's not coming back – but it is usually because of that cute fling.

On the other hand, you have the ugly fling. When I say ugly, I don't mean unbearably ugly. I mean not as cute as you. This is what this chapter's question is all about. You may have been cheated on, and then you saw the girl on "Facebook" or "My Space" and your mouth dropped because you were wondering, "What in the world?" This is what I call the ugly fling. This is the girl that either knows your man has a girl and doesn't care (and believes she can take your place) or is looking for a man very desperately. When a man cheats down, it's usually because he is just bored and wondering if he still has it. He is wondering what it's like to be with another woman again. Sometimes that woman is just ugly to another woman, but the man could see something completely different when he's looking at her. I mentioned in another chapter that a man may cheat because of one thing; that one thing could be virtually anything. It could be her car, her eyes, her apartment, her legs, her breasts, or any one particular thing. As a whole, that woman may not be as cute as you, but in that one area she is way cuter than you. She may have imperfect teeth, or she may have short hair, and so you deemed her as not cute. Nonetheless she may have a butt like J-Lo, and that's all your man was seeing. The rest really didn't matter because he just wanted to see what she looked like in a thong or butt naked, so that's why he went with her. Remember, a man won't leave you for another woman unless she is an upgrade. She has to be better than you as a whole, not just in one area. On the other hand, when it comes to cheating, all she has to have is one thing that you don't have.

If the girl is truly not cute, and there is nothing about her that is cute, and you as a girlfriend or wife are not being biased, then most likely he just was doing it just to do it. As sad as it may sound, sometimes we do it just to do it. When it's over, we even question ourselves as to why we did it or if it was it worth it, and the answer is oftentimes, "No." Nonetheless, we've already done it. Now that the deed is done, there is no going back. Now, we may think twice before we repeat it, but there will come a time when we venture down that ugly road again. As women, you can rest assured that your man will always come back from that encounter and, unless you leave him, he won't stop. Most of the time when a man cheats down it's because there is something he wants to test or something he wants to find out, so that girl is like an experiment, in a sense. If a man who is handsome messes with a girl who is not cute, you can almost bet your bottom dollar it took little or no effort for him to do so. Therefore, his test or night of fun took nothing out of him and is easy to do over and over again. At the same time, he may be trying to send you a message. He might know that you will find out, ask why he did it, and still be with him, so he does it to make you step your game up. He does it to let you know he can do it and to show you that you still don't have his heart. Therefore, as a woman, you have no room for complacency. If you are complacent, this attitude becomes the reinforcement for him to do this same thing to you over and over again. After a while, this will become very belittling and this will demoralize you in such a way that it may take a very long time to regain your self-esteem.

A downgrade is easy any way you look at it. It doesn't take much to do and means little to him. An upgrade is what takes time, and that is what takes effort. It is better to know he is *cheating down* rather than trying to *cheat up*—even though neither one is good!

So I ask you : "Have you ever been cheated on? When your man cheated, did he cheat up or down? After he cheated, did you remain in that relationship? If he cheated down, how did it make you feel? After he cheated up, how did it make you feel? Do you know if he cheated up or down?"

All of those questions are important to ask yourself, because how you respond to your man's cheating will determine if, when, or how he will cheat again. If he cheats down, and you stay with him, what message does that send him? If he cheats, and you step up your game, what message does that send him? Either way, if you stay, you are sending a message that will end up your worst enemy. I've cheated on women before and then made it known to them in a confession session of some sort. A woman never left me because of my cheating, and I know a lot of women who stay in relationships after they have been cheated on. This only reinforces that man's behavior, and it empowers him to do the same thing over and over again. Therefore, you have to rock the boat, in a sense, in order to see a change in his behavior and improvement in the relationship. I do not believe there is much a woman can do to stop a man from cheating, but I do believe there are some things a woman can do to divert his cheating scheme. If your man has cheated down, and you were blown away wondering why, flip the script and see if ugly is what he wants. Of course, you know it's not, but it will send him in another direction. If your man has cheated, then, instead of stepping up, step down. After he has cheated, and you are made aware of this, go from Miss Beautiful to Miss Hideous. Wear sweat pants and big tee shirts. Don't do your hair or your make up and force him to look at you. When he wants to take you out to make up for his infidelity, go out looking like you just got out of bed. Since he is the one who made the mistake, he will have to accept you just as you are. This will send him in the wrong direction. To him you will seem like you are torn apart and maybe you are, but, instead of hiding it, let him know exactly how you feel. Show the other side, the not so perfect and beautiful side. Then, when he asks why you are dressing that way, and why you don't fix yourself up, tell him you thought he liked uglier girls. Unfortunately, a lot of women do the opposite and don't realize that this reinforces a man's cheating habits. If your man sees that cheating pulls you away from him and makes you take greater pride in yourself and causes you to step up your game, this will cause him to slow his promiscuous behavior. Next time, he will think before he tries to cheat.

Whether it's up or down, if you stay with a man after he has cheated then most likely he'll continue to do it. I know you may be in too deep to leave, and you may just say you don't care and live like that. When you do that, you will push him away, and then you are asking to be replaced. When you begin to find that complacency, then he'll start to cheat up looking for your replacement. When a man cheats, and it is with a woman who is not cute, he probably isn't looking to leave you. He is just looking for a fling. If you wish to stop it, then you have to become more involved in his life and keep him on edge when it comes to your intimacy with him. Try new things and *be his freak* every now and then. When you want to keep your man to yourself, you have to be his everything. You have to be his stripper, his porn star, his video girl, and his runway model. Push the bar and force yourself to grow and step outside of your comfort zone. That way, you won't have to worry as much about him fulfilling lust with ugly girls because he can fulfill them with you. When it all boils down to it, it's up to you. You can keep your man home more, and you can keep him out of the ugly girl's (and cute girls) pot of goodies if you allow him to get all he wants out of yours.

To reiterate, the reason a man cheats with an ugly girl is because he is looking to fulfill a lust or to send a message and see if he can do it. In most cases, an ugly girl cannot be a threat to your relationship. You'll never see a man leave a swan for an ugly duckling. But he will use the ugly duckling to make the swan jealous and make the swan question herself in ways that asks, "Am I not that pretty?" or, "Is she as pretty as me?" A lot of men have goals to demoralize you, to make you think he is all you can have and that outside of him you have no hope. This assures him that you won't leave him, because in his mind, he has yours. As long as you think that you are not even pretty enough to keep him home, then he knows you won't ever think you're pretty enough to leave. I know when that happens, that makes you question yourself about who you are and what you look like, and that is the worst thing you can do. Never question yourself when your man decides to step outside of the relationship. That is often viewed as a basic characteristic of being a man, and he does that no matter who you are, what you look like, or how you dress. A man will be a man. Every man has cheated down at one time or another, and, out of the ten men I asked why they did it, they all said they just did it for the heck of it. Once again, that proved my theory to be right, which is that cheating never meant anything beyond the adventure. The only time a man will cheat up is when he is ready to leave. As long as you can find out he is cheating and you know that she isn't as pretty as you, just know it's meant to demoralize you and force you to step up or step out. What will you do if (or the next time) it happens to you?

CHAPTER 10

What Can Stop A Man From Cheating?

W*hat Daddy Never Told His Little Girl*, didn't have this chapter, but, now that I've grown to this point in my life, I can write about it. So many women are looking for that one true love. The sad thing is, not many women find him. Throughout this book, I've revealed an awful lot about a man. I've given you the truth, the whole truth, and nothing but the truth. Now, your question is, "Is there any hope?" My answer is, "Yes! " A man can be faithful, but it only comes at a certain point in his life. A point in his life when he has found a foundation that is bigger, stronger and able to carry him through difficult times in his life. A point when he believes in something greater than himself. A point when he has strict moral standards in his life. This is the time of a man's life in which he can be faithful.

I'll dive a little deeper into what I've just said. Imagine a man who drinks, smokes and curses. Not only that, but he may club hop from time to time. On top of that, he may sell drugs or deal in organized crime for a living. This man has no real sense of morals. By many accounts, he is an outlaw. He is deviant and defiant. He goes against the norms of society in every way he possibly can. Now, ask yourself: "If he doesn't care about his life or the law of the land, then why would he care about me? What would stop him from cheating on me?"

On the other hand, imagine a man who lives his life for God. This man is one who goes to church every Sunday and is a role model for the youth. This man doesn't drink, smoke, or curse; instead his body is a temple and he seeks wisdom and knowledge. This man has a strong sense of morals, mainly because he is living his life for God, and God's word teaches against fornication and adultery. This man isn't just concerned with loving you, he is also concerned with loving God. He understands that he has to account for his actions and his short comings. He knows God is real, so he understands that even when you can't see him, God can. So, he lives his life for Christ, and by doing that he is living the best life he can for you.

My father told me as I was growing up, "Son, the only way a man can be faithful to a woman is if he is rooted and grounded in the word of God". For some time I didn't completely understand what he was saying. As I grew older, I began to understand exactly what he was saying. I understood that he was speaking from a grown man's and Pastor perspective. I grew to realize that he was right. I saw myself fall short in so many relationships because I was relying on my own set of morals and my own strength. I came to realize that I needed strength from God. As I began to pray for strength, I noticed it immediately. I grew to love the Lord, and I feared his wrath. Even when my wife made me angry, or if I was curious about other women, God kept me strong. I was so afraid of him taking his Grace and Mercy from my life, I remained faithful. I often tell my wife, "Baby I'm faithful, not just because of you, but because of my love for the Lord and my fear and respect for Him." I knew that I needed his blessings over my life. I could see the way he opened up doors and put me on platforms for my voice to be heard, and I knew he was honoring my obedience and faithfulness.

All my life, I have never met a faithful man unless he was a man of God. The men of God were the only men who even had a remote chance of being faithful, and even then we see some fall short. I am convinced that if God can't keep a man, then nothing can. I know God can keep a man if that man earnestly wants to be kept. God can grant me the strength, but if I don't want to respect the strength then it won't benefit me. I'll just be a strong man cheating. I want the strength of God over my life. I yearn for the strength of the Lord, I long for it. I get on my knees and I pray with everything in me that he keeps me faithful, and thus far he hasn't let me down.

Of course, I understand that every man isn't a religious man, and every woman isn't a religious woman. Therefore, for you, I would say make sure your man is latched onto something in his life that is bigger than him. Make sure your man has dreams and goals and ambitions that would make him look bad if he got caught cheating on you. Examples would be a leader, a cop, a teacher, a role model, a lawyer, a doctor, or something of status. Understand that if your man is in illegal activity, then his sense of morals isn't against cheating. Cheating is nothing to him; he is more worried about getting caught and going to prison. Cheating actually comes with the lifestyle of a thug. You aren't seen as a real thug if you're whipped by one woman. If you don't have enough money to have more than one woman, then you aren't even respected in the field. So many women date criminal minded men, and they put up with the "thug passion" and "thug love," but they hurt and cry when they find out he is cheating – as if it is a surprise to them.

I'm here to let every woman know that if your man doesn't have a strong sense of morals, then that should be the first sign to let you know that he won't be faithful to you. I've been on the other side. I've been in the streets; I know what the lifestyle is like. I know about the flash, the glitz, and the glam. The fast money attracts fast women. A man's stress level is so high when he's in the streets that sometimes he needs something new, a new voice, a new smile, and a new touch. Many men in that lifestyle long for other women, just because he thinks it helps to fortify his manhood. It goes deeper than the fast money and fast women. It's about the thrill and the rush. Men are a competitive species. That is why so many men live the life of crime – because of the thrill. The rush that we get when we know we are getting over on the law. The feeling we get when we know we are making more money than the teachers who put us down in school or the cops who are harassing us in the streets. That's a rush and a thrill that many men long to experience. A 9-to-5 isn't enough for him. That is why almost every man you know plays some type of sport; we are competitors. If he doesn't play sports, then he plays video games or cards or board games. He's doing that to feed a craving for a thrill, a craving for competition, which is exactly what cheating does. Cheating does the same exact thing. A man gets a rush when he can tell you he is going to play ball with the boys or going to hit a lick, but instead he goes to another girl's apartment and gets with her. Then he comes home that same night with a value meal or a sweaty shirt to throw you off, then he sleeps with you! That is a thrill like none other. At that point in time, that man feels like a king. That man feels like the pimps he sees on TV. He feels invincible. He feels unstoppable, like he has the world in the palm of his hand. It's a thrill.

On the other hand, you may have the unreligious man who is a major athlete. He plays for a Division I school, or he is a professional in his sport of choice. Many women long for these types of men because they want a better life. They want to be able to buy whatever they want. They want to be on TV under his arm. They want the quick money to finance their own dreams. For whatever reason, millions of women long for a man in the limelight. Not many realize what they are getting themselves into. They don't realize that the money won't take away the pain they will feel when they find out that he has been unfaithful to them. They don't realize that his lifestyle beckons many women to him. In the entertainment world, cheating is accepted and expected for the most part. We see every day another sex scandal in the media with some celebrity. It's expected. For some reason, many women believe they can be *the* woman to change that man or that their man is different from the rest. Then one day they realize that he is no different from the rest. They realize that he is human just like the other men they see in the news. At that point, the Gucci, Dolce,

Jimmy Choo, Fendi, or whatever designer she may have in her closet can't take away the pain. The money can't wipe away the tears. She realizes then that what she is lacking in that relationship money can't buy. She realizes that she didn't need a million-dollar man to buy the Charmin tissue consoling her in her loneliest moments.

I've known girlfriends of star athletes or just professional athletes. I never met one among them that was content. The reason being that none of their athletic other halves were God-fearing men. They were regular, average men depending on themselves. Depending on their own strength, the strength that got them to where they are in life. They were so consumed with themselves and their status and accolades that they could care less about how the woman felt. They didn't take the time to hear her out or respect her dreams. They came up like average men, so using that platform they took advantage of it. They conquered every woman they could. They went with every woman that came their way because they weren't used to it. And, even if they were, they hadn't had enough of it. They wanted more. They wanted all they could get. They were human. They were just like every other man who didn't fear God. "They were mere men". Some women put up with it. Some women are content with the money; they feel, "At least, if I'm going to get mistreated, I'll be rich at the same time." What some didn't realize is that they were disposable. They didn't realize that when that man was tired of them, he would up and leave and go to the next woman. At that point, they were left without pride and dignity and nowhere to turn because they didn't love themselves enough to get out earlier. They figured they would stick it out, but instead they got stuck out!

A man who is a leader, a teacher, a cop, a lawyer, a doctor, a government official, these men have a chance of being faithful. The reason being is they have too much to lose. They are in the public eye, and they know that if they are caught in a cheating scandal they will never live it down. They know it's against the law to cheat in a marriage and that they are sworn into their position and have to uphold the law. STILL, even with all the status and all the power and respect, we have seen so many fall short. We have watched them over and over in the media after being caught in sex scandals of every kind. I won't call any names at all because their names aren't important; but instead I simply want to point out that they are human. I'm also looking at the fact that they are men, the fact that they fell short even when they were in the public eye.

As a woman, you shouldn't be naïve or gullible. Take it exactly for what it is, THE TRUTH! I come in contact with so many women who say, "Oh, not my man." Sooner or later, they come back and say, "You were right, he is only a man." I'm not bashing men because I'm a man. I'm saying that a man without the strength of God operating in his life can't be the man that you want or need. So, as a woman you should take heed to the warning signs that are before you and don't feel like you are any more special than any other woman. Know that your man needs a foundation and a belief system that is bigger than him, and, without it, you will get disappointed just like so many other women you know.

I don't want to offend anyone. I don't want to step on any toes either. I am a devout Christian, but I've also been a star athlete. I've been a drug dealer. I've owned my own business. I've been in the limelight. I've been through all the stages, and I AM CONVINCED of one thing. ONLY THE

STRENGTH FROM GOD can keep a man faithful. I know that at no point in my life was I faithful until I came into the knowledge of the Lord. At no point in my life was I faithful until I used the strength that only God can give a man. Even men who seem to operate in this strength have fallen short, but that's because they weren't using it. They weren't tapped into it. They allowed their flesh to get the best of them. They wanted that sin at that time, with the hopes that God would forgive them.

I'm at a point in my life where I won't test God. The Bible says that "Thou shall not tempt the Lord thy God." That means don't try his Grace and Mercy when you know better. That means do everything in your power to stay in right standing with the Lord thy God at all times, not just when convenient. This book isn't only for Christians; it's for real people, and God is real. I've been on both sides of the line. I've experienced my own strength, and it failed me; and I've experienced the strength of God, and it sustained me.

Women ought to seek out or wait on a man who is a God-fearing man. Wait on a man who can tell you what his last devotional reading was, a man who can go to church with you on Sunday, a man who claims and professes the strength of God in his life. Ladies, this is real! I'm a living witness. I'm a faithful man to my wife because I'm walking with God and not on my own. I am under constant attack by the devil because of my statements in this book; and because I've stepped out on the word of God – the devil wants to make me eat my words! He sends the prettiest women across my path to tempt me. He makes it easy for me, he sends me opportunities that I didn't have when I was single and looking for love. Now that I've proclaimed God's words and called him out, the devil is testing me daily. I can't sit back and relax, I can't have a weak day. I can't go to sleep angry with my wife, God won't allow it. I must stay prayed up and read up more than ever because now I've proclaimed my strength. Women read this book and throw themselves at me just to see if I live what I preach. Just to see if I've really grown past this so that I can teach about it. They want to know if I'm really faithful. They say if you are faithful then my man can be faithful, too. If that is you, then just make sure your man is living the lifestyle that I'm living, which is a God-fearing man. I bask in the presence of the Lord. I pray all day for strength. I sleep on it. I eat on it. I drink on it, and I believe in it. If you want your man to be faithful, then lead him to the Lord!

Note From The Author

Thank you for reading this book. I hope that it empowers you in your relationships with men. Please take the things you've read and implement them in your life. Keep your head up and know that the only good man is one whom you love sincerely; and who loves *you* sincerely as well. Elevate your lifestyle, elevate your relationship.

I am currently compiling scenario questions about relationships that will be included in an upcoming book. If you have a scenario question that requires further discussion or a specific response, please contact me without hesitation.

Contact me at:
www. whatdaddynevertold.com
tagaskin@mail. usf. edu
213-814-0456

Interviews, book signings, or guest appearances can also be arranged.

BE BLESSED!

Special Thanks To:

First, I would like to thank God for being with me and gracing this project. I would like to say thanks to my wife, Sheri Chanroo Gaskins, for supporting this work and not holding all that she has read against me. I knew that if I were with a weak woman, she would leave me over a book like this. However, my wife stood by my side, and not only understood, but had a hand in making this book complete. I want to say thanks to my homie, Alex Dukes, for inspiring parts of the book and adding insight to my life. R. I. P. homie, you are missed. Next, I would like to thank Joslyn Giles for sparking the conversation, which led me to writing this book. I appreciate the encouragement, Joslyn. I would also like to thank Andrea Woodfolk for coming up with the wonderful title of the first rendition of this book. Andrea, you were a much-needed inspiration. I couldn't have come up with a title like that without you. Thank you, Gewanda Johnson, my beautiful and brilliant cousin. Thanks, Gewan, for your response to the chapter I sent you. I value your opinion very much. I would like to thank my little sister, Latesha Gaskins, for proofreading the book and giving me honest feedback. I love you, Tesha. I thank my Momma also for bringing me in this world and supporting everything I want to do in life. I also would like to thank my best friend and CEO/Founder of Krosstown Productions for designing the cover of my first book. Tiger, I can always count on you to support whatever project I have in mind. I appreciate it more than you know. I would like to thank Wesley Barnett for his support in my dreams also. Wesley, you're a true friend. Last, and most importantly, I would like to thank my father, Tony A. Gaskins Sr., for guiding my life and teaching me all that I know and training my mind to think outside of the box and teaching me how to articulate the feelings of my heart. Daddy, I love you so much and I appreciate everything you have done for me. If there was a definition for tough love, your picture would be beside it. You are truly the man that I admire the most. THANK YOU ALL!